Exploring Parks
with
Ranger Dockett

Written by
ALICE K. FLANAGAN

Photographs by
CHRISTINE OSINSKI

Reading Consultant
LINDA CORNWELL
Learning Resource Consultant
Indiana Department of Education

CHILDREN'S PRESS®   *A Division of Grolier Publishing*
New York • London • Hong Kong • Sydney • Danbury, Connecticut

Special thanks to Michael Dockett
for allowing us to tell his story.

The lighthouse on page seven is featured in the famous children's story
The Little Red Lighthouse and the Great Gray Bridge by Hildegard H. Swift
and Lynd Ward, published by Harcourt Brace.

Library of Congress Cataloging-in-Publication Data
Flanagan, Alice.
   Exploring parks with Ranger Dockett / written by Alice K.
Flanagan; photographs by Christine Osinski ; reading consultant, Linda
Cornwell.
     p. cm. — (Our neighborhood)
   Summary: Follows an urban park ranger as he tends to the ponds,
fountains, plants, and animals in his care and teaches people about the
parks that form an exciting outdoor classroom.
    ISBN 0-516-20496-3 (lib bdg.)   0-516-26248-3 (pbk.)
    1. Park rangers—New York (State)—New York—Juvenile literature.
2. Park rangers—Vocational guidance—New York (State)—New York—
Juvenile literature. 3. Parks—New York (State)—New York—Juvenile
literature. [1. Park rangers. 2. Parks. 3. Occupations.] I. Osinski,
Christine, ill. II. Title. III. Series: Our neighborhood.
SB486.V62F53 1997
363.6′8—dc21   97-4125
                                                 CIP
                                                 AC

Photographs ©: Christine Osinski

Right in the middle of busy New York City is a wide, wonderful park.

It is one of many parks that
Ranger Dockett takes care of as
an Urban Park Ranger.

Each day, he has many tasks. He takes visitors on bird-watching walks.

And he gives special tours of the parks.

Sometimes, he talks about the statues along the paths. There's Christopher Columbus and Alice in Wonderland with the Mad Hatter!

On his long walks through the city parks, Ranger Dockett keeps in touch with other rangers.

Together, they make sure everyone follows the rules . . .

. . . to keep the parks safe and clean.

Ranger Dockett does
his best to make each
park a safe place . . .

. . . where people can walk or play.

Every day, Ranger Dockett teaches people how to care for the special green spaces in the heart of the city.

He shows them how to protect the plants and animals that live there.

Each year, he plants young trees.

He explains how important they are to the park habitat.

Sometimes, he
teaches classes
at the pond.

20

He talks about the plant life at the water's edge.

His students look for turtles, frogs, and insects.

Ranger Dockett puts on special boots.

Carefully, he wades to the middle of the pond with his net.

When he brings back mud from the
bottom of the pond, everyone
searches for signs of life.

Will they find a beetle or a dragonfly?

Look! There's a snail!

Ranger Dockett was a Boy Scout when he was a little boy. Later, he went to school to learn how to be a ranger.

Ever since then, he has been exploring nature with others.

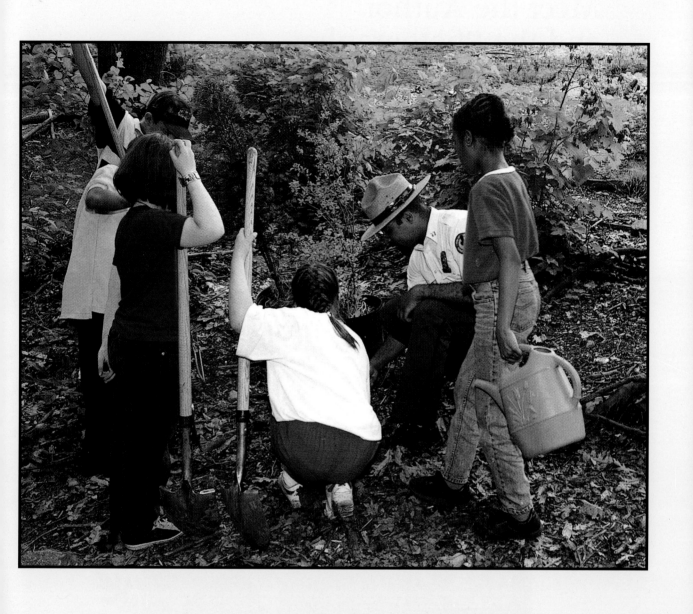

The park is his exciting classroom!

Meet the Author
and the Photographer

Alice Flanagan and Christine Osinski are sisters. They grew up together telling stories and drawing pictures in a brown brick bungalow in a southwest-side neighborhood of Chicago, Illinois. Today they write stories and take photographs professionally.

Ms. Flanagan resides in Chicago with her husband and works as a freelance writer. Ms. Osinski is a photographer and teaches at The Cooper Union for the Advancement of Science and Art in New York City. She lives with her husband and two sons on Staten Island.

01/02/98